RICH THOMPSON · ALEX HOKAMP · BLAKE TURNER · BILL GRACE · BUSTER STEWARD · FRED HUNT · HARRY MAYO · PINKY PEDEMONTE

SANTA CRUZ SURFING CLUB
JUNE 1941

sURFINg

SURFING
SURFING
SURFING

Nancy N. Schiffer
in cooperation with
The San Francisco Airport Museums

Douglas Congdon-Martin, photographer

Schiffer Publishing Ltd

4880 Lower Valley Road, Atglen, PA 19310 USA

Schiffer, Nancy.
    Surfing, surfing, surfing / Nancy N. Schiffer in cooperation
with the San Francisco Airport Museums ; Douglas Congdon-
Martin, photographer.
        p.   cm.
    ISBN 0-7643-0655-3
    1. Surfing--Hawaii. 2. Surfing--Hawaii--Pictorial works. 3.
Surfing--California, Southern. 4. Surfing--California,
Southern--Pictorial works. 5. Surfing--California, Northern.
6. Surfing--California, Northern--Pictorial works. I. Congdon-
Martin, Douglas. II. Title.
GV840.S82H387   1998
797.3'2'09794--dc21   98-28709
                                                       CIP

Design by Blair Loughrey
Type set in Adlib BT/Futura BK BT

ISBN: 0-7643- 0655-3
Printed in China

Published by Schiffer Publishing Ltd.
4880 Lower Valley Road
Atglen, PA 19310
Phone: (610) 593-1777; Fax: (610) 593-2002
E-mail: Schifferbk@aol.com
Please write for a free catalog.
This book may be purchased from the publisher.
Please include $3.95 for shipping.

In Europe, Schiffer books are distributed by
Bushwood Books
6 Marksbury Avenue
Kew Gardens
Surrey TW9 4JF England
Phone: 44(0)181-392-8585; Fax: 44(0) 181-392-9876
E-mail: Bushwd@aol.com

Please try your bookstore first.

We are interested in hearing from authors
with book ideas on related subjects.

CONTENTS

ACKNOWLEDGMENTS

The San Francisco Airport Commission initiated the Exhibitions Program in 1980. Exhibitions are organized in the three Airport terminals by the San Francisco Airport Museums. Technical support is provided by the Corporation of The Fine Arts Museums of San Francisco.

The exhibition *He'e Nalu: Wave Riding* was presented in the North Terminal Connector Gallery from October, 1997 to February, 1998.

Thanks to:

Ross Adami
Tom Adler
Scott Anderson
W. Babcock / Angels, Carpinteria, Calif.
Dr. J. H. Ball
Art Brewer
L. T. Caywoody
J. & M. Ford, Oakland, Calif.
LeRoy Grannis
The Keating Family
Wayne Levin
Lee Nichol
Laura and Greg Noll and Family

O'Neill
Jay Novak
Jerry Pierce
Dan Pincetich
Mark Renneker, M.D.
Santa Cruz Surfing Museum
Gary Saxon - The Record Man
John Schell
John Sherry
C. R. Stecyk
Cary B. Weiss
and all other lenders to the exhibition

INTRODUCTION

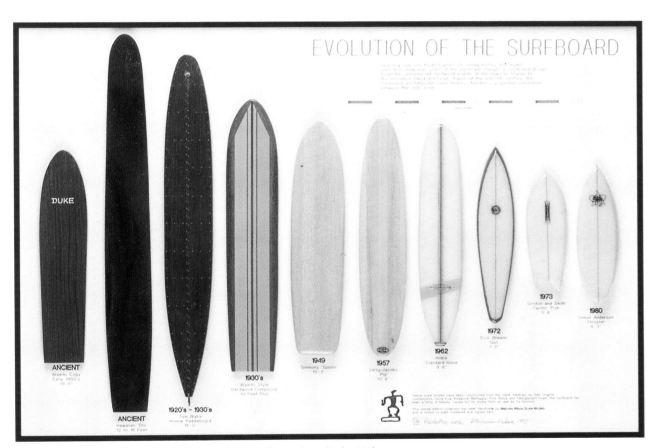

Evolution of the surfboard, Malcolm Wilson,
1993, mixed media. Collection of Dan Pincetich

Surfing has always had a distinct position in the coastal communities where it is practiced. At one time surfing was even reserved for kings. The *ali'i* (royalty) of Hawai`i used exclusive beaches for *he'e nalu* (wave sliding). Surfing is still a favorite water sport for many men and women of all ages.

The ancient Polynesian heritage of surfing was introduced to the western world by Hawaiians such as Duke Kahanamoku in the early 1900s. In a later period surfing expanded internationally and a unique culture was created. Its popularity grew steadily in Calfornia during the 1950s and 1960s and surf culture was assimilated into a west coast lifestyle. The music, filmmaking, photography, design, and literature of surfing have all influenced popular culture. Its dialect and style of dress are widely emulated. Images of surfing as the epitome of California culture persist in the American mind.

Surfing's essence has always been the natural forces of the sea and the surfer's adaptation to its conditions. Surfboards have evolved from 150-pound solid redwood boards to the "hollow" surfboards pioneered by Tom Blake in 1928 at Waikiki to the lightweight foam and fiberglass boards of the 1970s. Northern California's unique contribution was an adaptation to the water temperature: at 45 degrees surfers could not be comfortable for long nor in winter. In the early 1960s Jack O'Neill developed the wetsuit at Ocean Beach, San Francisco. As a result, the endless summer could be found on any beach in the world.

"Famous Surf Riders, Nov. 5, 1911," paper. Collection of Dan Pincetich

> "A surfer takes only the barest minimum of equipment into the sea and prevails—not by opposing but by joining a wave."
>
> George Leonard, *The Ultimate Athlete*, 1974

"Floating," 1983, Wayne Levin, gelatin silver print. ©Wayne Levin

"Body Surfers," 1983, Wayne Levin, gelatin silver print. ©Wayne Levin

"Waves are an endless source of fascination for everyone, from scientists to surfers. Who, in watching, is not mesmerized by the ongoing cycles of surge and rush, flow and ebb, storm and calm?"

Drew Kampion, *The Book of Waves*, 1989

"Diving Under," 1992,
Wayne Levin, gelatin silver
print. ©Wayne Levin

9

"Kicking Out," 1996,
Wayne Levin, gelatin silver
print. ©Wayne Levin

10

Surfing Hawai`i

Simple surfboarding—in which a swimmer used a short plank or other aid to ride a wave just for the fun of it—has been practiced for thousands of years throughout Polynesia, that great triangle of islands bounded by Hawai`i in the north, Easter Island in the southeast, and New Zealand in the southwest. Originally a children's pastime practiced with short bodyboards, it was taken up by adult men and women on the main islands of East Polynesia using larger boards. Finally, along the shores of the Hawaiian islands, the art of standing up on the big board while riding diagonally across a wave front reached its peak. In 1778 Lieutenant James King, logkeeper for the Pacific expedition of British explorer Captain James Cook, wrote of Hawaiian surfers: "Their first object is to place themselves on the summit of the largest surge, by which they are driven with amazing rapidity towards shore." Beginning in 1821, surfing was almost completely eliminated by European Christian missionaries, who considered it an immoral form of amusement and suppressed it along with much else in the Hawaiian culture. By the time surfing was revived around the turn of the twentieth century, there were only a handful of Hawaiian surfers left.

"Outrigger canoe and surfer at Waikiki Beach with Diamond Head in the background." Collection of John H. Hill

"...cherubic faced, with a thatch of curly yellow hair...his body was hugely thewed as a Hercules, while above him, ten feet at least, upreared a wall of overtopping water...[he] sprang to meet the blow, and, just when it seemed he must be crushed, he dived into the face of the breaker and disappeared."

Jack London, *The Valley of the Moon*, 1913

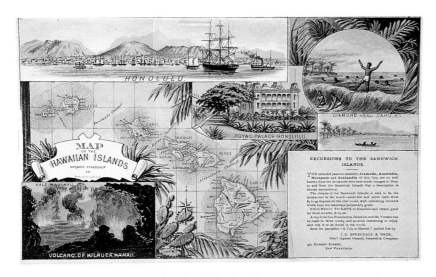

Above and right: Color brochure, "Oceanic Steamship Co.," printed paper. Collection of J. & M. Ford

Color postcard, "2 Surfboard Riders of Hawaii - The Sport of Kings," Sydney Short Line. Collection of J. & M. Ford

Color postcard, paper.
Collection of Dan Pincetich

Color postcard, "Surf Board Riding, Honolulu, TH." Collection of J. & M. Ford

Above & left: Adzes, stone. Collection of J. & M. Ford

Poi pounder, stone. Collection of J. & M. Ford

14

Kukui nut lei.
Collection of J. & M.
Ford

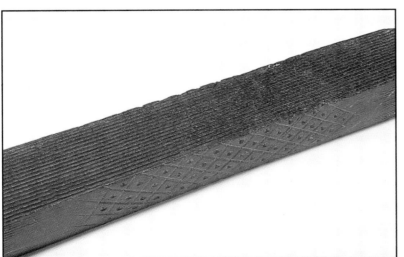

Above: Tapa beaters, hardwood.
Collection of J. & M. Ford.

Left: Detail of a tapa beater,
hardwood. Collection of J. & M.
Ford

15

Above & right: Calabashes, koa wood. Collection of J. & M. Ford

16

Photograph of Queen Kapi'olani, gelatin
silver print. Collection of J. & M. Ford

Photograph of King David Kalakaua, c. 1890,
gelatin silver print. Collection of J. & M. Ford

Photograph of Princess Lili'uokalani, c. 1890,
gelatin silver print. Collection of J. & M. Ford

17

Surfboards

The board used in surfing has developed from a 150-pound, cigar-shaped, handcarved wooden longboard used by Hawaiians in the nineteenth century to today's lightweight mass produced surf boards made of fiberglass and polyurethane foam.

With its traditional, or ancient, shape this *alaia* style surfboard was used for riding in a prone or standing position most often on waves breaking close to shore. The scarcity of the Hawaiian koa wood and other native Hawaiian woods led to an increased use of redwood from the Mainland. c. 1915, redwood. Collection of Dan Pincetich

"Surfrider - Waikiki," framed drypoint on paper, 1918, H. M. Luquiens. Collection of Dan Pincetich

"The higher the sea and the larger the waves, in their opinion the better the sport. On these occasions they use a board, which they call *papa he'e nalu* (wave sliding board), generally five or six feet long, and rather more than a foot wide, sometimes flat, but more frequently slightly convex on both sides...When they reach the outside of the rocks, where the waves first break, they adjust themselves on one end of the board, lying flat on their faces, and watch the approach of the largest billow; they then poise themselves on its highest edge, and, paddling as it were with their hands and feet, ride on the crest of the wave, in the midst of the spray and the foam, till within a yard or two of the rocks or the shore; and when the observers would expect to see them dashed to pieces, they steer with great address between the rocks, or slide off their board in a moment, grasp it by the middle, and dive under the water, while the wave rolls on, and breaks among the rocks with roaring noise, the effect of which is greatly heightened by the shouts and laughter of the natives in the water."

William Ellis, "Hawaiian Surfing in the 1820s," 1831

Kelea-The Surf Rider, A Romance of Pagan Hawaii, A.S. Twombly, 1900, printed paper. Collection of Mark Renneker, M.D.

Left: "Surfer," framed drypoint on paper, 1920, H. M. Luquiens. Collection of Dan Pincetich

Below: "Surf Riders," drypoint on paper, 1920, H. M. Luquiens. Collection of Dan Pincetich

Color postcard. Collection
of Dan Pincetich

Postcard, "Surfboard Riding at Waikiki Beach,
Honolulu, Hawaii." Collection of J. & M. Ford

"Surfriders, Honolulu," Ambrose Patterson, wood block
print on paper. Collection of Dan Pincetich

20

Color postcard, "#233 Famous Surf Board Riders,
Hawaiian Islands." Collection of J. & M. Ford

Color postcard, "H-172 Surf Riding, Waikiki."
Collection of J. & M. Ford

Color postcard, "Surf Riding, Hawaii."
Collection of J. & M. Ford

"I tried surf-bathing once...but made a failure of it. I got the
board placed right, and at the right moment, too; but missed
the connection myself. The board struck the shore in three-quar-
ters of a second, without any cargo, and I struck the bottom
about the same time, with a couple of barrels of water in me.
None but natives ever master the art of surf-bathing thoroughly."

Mark Twain, 1872

New marine glues developed during World War I were used to laminate redwood sections together which added strength and integrity to surfboards. This example was re-shaped decades later by Dale Velzy, late 1920s, redwood. Collection of Dan Pincetich

Color postcard, "A Daring Surf Board Rider, Honolulu, T.H." Collection of J. & M. Ford

Color postcard, "Sport in the Surf, Honolulu, T.H." Collection of J. & M. Ford

Above & left: Home made and decorated with a burnt wood surf-rider motif, this *paipo* style "body board," or "belly board," was used for shore break by children or adults in medium to small surf. The bottom contour increased the rider's ability to steer, 1920-1930, redwood. Collection of Cary B. Weiss

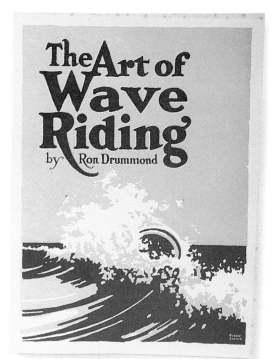

The Art of Wave Riding, Ron Drummond, 1931, printed paper. Collection of Mark Renneker, M.D.

"Uncle Dick" Keating at Waikiki while training for the Olympic Trials, 1930s, gelatin silver print. Collection of The Keating Family

Above & facing page: Basic rental surfboards at Waikiki Beach were available for tourists who wanted to try surfing during their visit to Hawai`i. The cut out tail design is a traditional shape and provided extra "bite" for controlling direction, 1930s, "Waikiki Rental," spruce. Collection of C. R. Stecyk

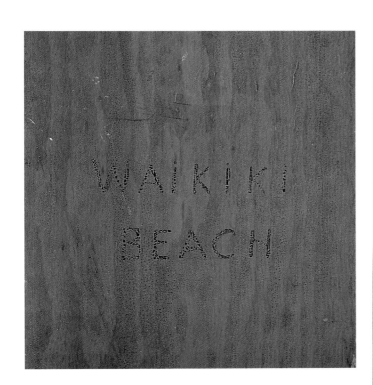

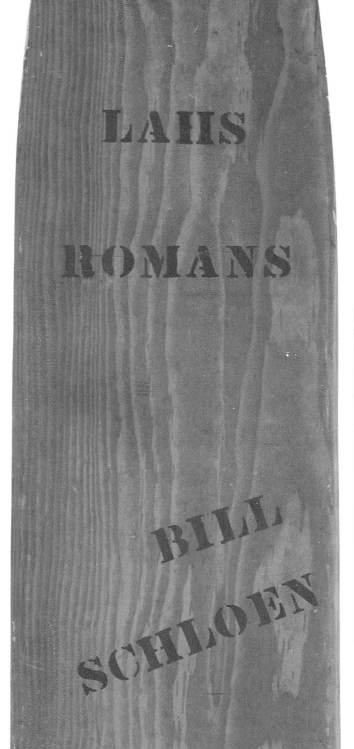

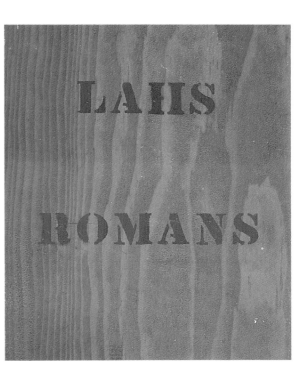

Color postcard, "Surfer Standing on Head." Collection of J. & M. Ford

Far left: Miniature surfboard, 1930s, koa wood. Collection of Cary B. Weiss

Left: Miniature surfboard with aloha decal, redwood. Collection of Dan Pincetich

"...necessary work for the maintenance of the family, such as farming, fishing, mat and tapa making, and such other household duties required of them and needing attention...was often neglected for the prosecution of the sport."

Anonymous writer, *Hawaiian Annual,* 1896

Surf-riding in Outrigger Canoe, Honolulu, T. H.

Color postcard, "Surfing - Waikiki Beach." Collection of J. & M. Ford

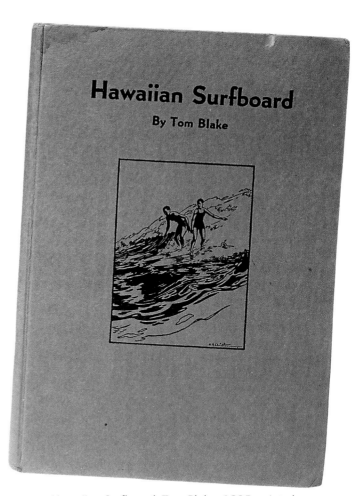

Miniature surfboard, redwood.
Collection of Dan Pincetich

Color postcard, "Surf Board
Riding, Hawaii," 1916.
Collection of J. & M. Ford

Color postcard, "Surfriding
at Waikiki, Honolulu," 1910.
Collection of J. & M. Ford

Hawaiian Surfboard, Tom Blake, 1935, printed
paper. Collection of Mark Renneker, M.D.

Pacific System Homes, Inc., a home-building company in Los Angeles, introduced the first commercially built surfboards in the 1930s. The redwood and pine sections were put together with tongue and groove joinery. Pacific System Homes, Inc., "Waikiki Surfboard," 1930-1940, redwood, pine. Collection of Jerry Pierce

"But tomorrow, ah, tomorrow, I shall be out in that wonderful water, and I shall come in standing up...And if I fail tomorrow, I shall do it the next day, or the next. Upon one thing I am resolved: the *Snark* shall not sail from Honolulu until I, too, wing my heels with the swiftness of the sea, and become a sunburned, skin-peeling Mercury."

Jack London, 1907

These commercially produced surfboards of the mid-1930s were a marked improvement over solid wood models. Pine and balsa wood reduced the weight while redwood rail, tails, and noses retained durability. Marine varnish was used for waterproofing. Shallow fins, first introduced by Tom Blake in 1935 for increased stability, were added to the bottom of these surfboards which cost less than $40 at the time. Pacific System Homes, Inc., 1930s, redwood, pine. Collection of Dan Pincetich

VARIOUS STYLES OF HAWAIIAN SURF RIDING

Postcard, "Various Styles of Hawaiian Surf Riding." Collection of J. & M. Ford

Postcard, "Surfers." Collection of J. & M. Ford

Postcard, "Surfriding at Waikiki,
Honolulu." Collection of J. & M. Ford

Postcard, "3 Surfers." Collection of J. & M. Ford

Postcard, " Surf Riding
at Waikiki, Honolulu."
Collection of J. & M.
Ford

Postcard, "Surfer." Collection
of J. & M. Ford

SURF RIDING - HAWAII

Postcard, "Surf Riding - Hawaii."
Collection of J. & M. Ford

The use of hard redwood at the outer edges and lighter woods such as pine and balsa wood for the inner sections became a dominant design principle in surfboard making during the late 1930s and early 1940s. Pacific Systems Homes, Inc. sent the first non-Hawaiian built surfboard to the Islands. Pacific System Homes, Inc. with Hawaiian Crest, 1941, balsa wood, redwood and pine. Collection of Dan Pincetich

32

Postcard, "H.173 Surf Riding, Waikiki," 1940s. Collection of J. & M. Ford

Postcard, "H.171 Surfriding, Waikiki." Collection of J. & M. Ford

Postcard, "Surfriders Waikiki Beach, w498." Collection of J. & M. Ford

Thomas Rogers of Venice, California, started making hollow surfboards and paddle boards in 1931. The hollow paddle board had been invented and patented by his friend Tom Blake in the 1920s. They were constructed like an airplane wing with internal ribbing for strength. These lightweight and fast moving water craft were very popular for surfing and racing. They were also used for life saving. Rogers, "Hawaiian Paddle Board," 1930s-1940s, redwood, pine. Collection of Dan Pincetich

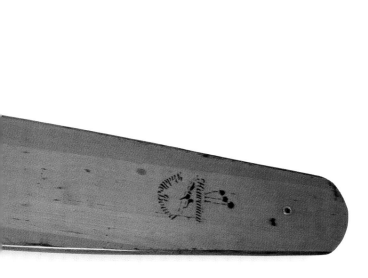

Color postcard, "Surf Riding at Waikiki,
Honolulu." Collection of J. & M. Ford

Postcard, "2 Surfers." Collection of J. & M. Ford

Ashtray, "Aloha Hawaii,"
Victoria Ceramics.
Collection of J. & M.
Ford

Souvenir
teaspoon,
1950s, metal.
Collection of
Dan Pincetich

Tableware with surfer: dinner plate, dessert plate,
and bowl, 1950s. Collection of Dan Pincetich

Souvenir teaspoon
and demitasse spoon,
1950s, metal.
Collection of Dan
Pincetich

Right: Miniature paddleboard, wood. Collection of Dan Pincetich

Fall right: Miniature surfboard, 1960, koa wood. Collection of Cary B. Weiss

Miniature Kahuna Classics surfboard, balsa wood. Collection of Dan Pincetich

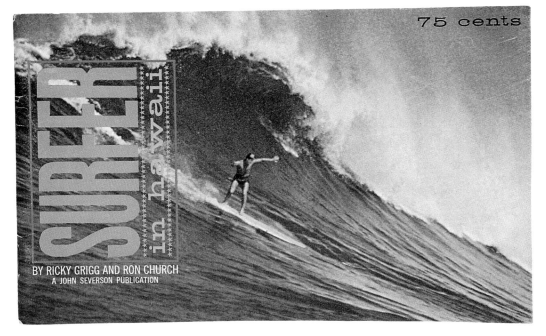

Self-bound booklet, *Surfer in Hawaii*, Grigg & Church, 1963, Printed paper. Collection of Cary B. Weiss

The original Inter-Island Surf Shop, located in Honolulu, Hawai`i, was opened by Mickey Lake in 1963. This child's surfboard combines redwood sections with a foam and balsa wood body. Inter-Island Surf Shop, 1964, foam, balsa wood, fiberglass. Collection of Dan Pincetich

Decal label for the
Inter-Island Surf Shop,
Hawai`i. Collection of
Cary B. Weiss

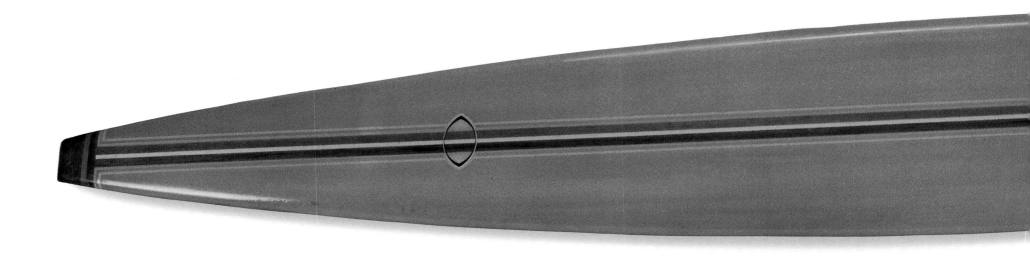

40

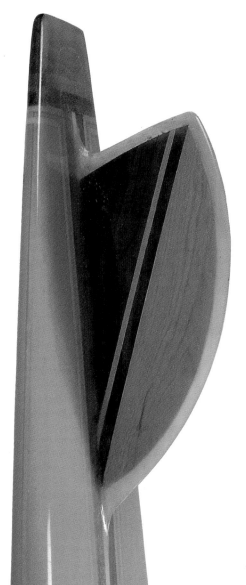

Modern surfboards specifically designed for riding the biggest waves were pioneered by surfer George Downing in Hawai'i during the 1950s. The nose and tail taper and elongated shape of these surfboards allowed a rider to "trim" at an angle along the steep face of a giant wave. As more Californians traveled to Hawai'i to challenge the big waves at Makaha Point and Sunset Beach, surfboard makers met the demand for new equipment. Bing Big Wave, 1964, foam, balsa wood, redwood, and fiberglass. Collection of Dan Pincetich

41

Right: Miniature surfboard labeled Hawaiian Island Creations. Collection of Dan Pincetich

Below: Miniature Bing surfboard, foam and wood. Collection of Dan Pincetich

"Surfriders, Honolulu," Charles W. Bartlett, wood block print on paper. Collection of Dan Pincetich

Shorter surfboards designed in the 1970s changed many aspects of surfing. Narrower boards with sharply turned-down rails kept the edges free and added speed. Surfers such as Gerry Lopez, noted for riding the Banzai Pipeline, were able to position themselves deeper in the tube, and generate enough speed to escape. Koplien Designs, 1976, foam, fiberglass. Collection of Cary B. Weiss

Competition

Californian and Hawaiian surfing traditions have remained closely allied ever since George Freeth, a surfer of Irish and Hawaiian ancestry, rode a solid wood board while visiting Redondo Beach, California in 1907, with California providing innovative materials and Hawai`i providing extraordinary surf in which to test new boards. Redwood from the mainland was imported in the early 1900s and used for solid "planks" and hollow boards. The hollow model of the 1920s was known as the Tom Blake board, after its inventor who was also credited with inventing the surfboard fin.

Postcard, "Duke Kahanamoku, Hawaiian Swimmer." Collection of J. & M. Ford

44

"Single Surfer, Duke Kahanamoku." Charles W. Bartlett,
wood block print on paper. Collection of Dan Pincetich

45

"I have never seen snow and do not know what winter means. I have never coasted down a hill of frozen rain, but every day of the year where the water is 76, day and night, and the waves roll high, I take my sled, without runners, and coast down the face of the big waves that roll in at Waikiki. How would you like to stand like a god before the crest of a monster billow, always rushing to the bottom of a hill and never reaching its base, and to come rushing in for half a mile at express speed, in a graceful attitude, of course, until you reach the beach and step easily from the wave to the strand?"

Duke Kahanamoku in *Waikiki Beachboy*, Grady Timmons, 1989

Makaha Surf Contest Program, 1956, paper. Collection of Dan Pincetich

Dick Keating "passport" to the 1967 Duke Kahanamoku Invitational Surfing Championships, 1967, printed paper. Collection of The Keating Family

Left: Aloha Days paddleboard race trophy, 1956, metal and plastic. Collection of Noll Family Trust, on loan to Rhyn Noll Surf Shop

Right: 1967 Duke Kahanamouku Invitational Surfing Championships trophy, won by Dick Keating in 1967, metal and wood. Collection of The Keating Family

Surf trunks from the 1967 Duke Kahanamoku Invitational Surfing Championships, 1967, fabric. Collection of The Keating Family

DUKE
KAHANAMOKU
INVITATIONAL
SURFING
CHAMPIONSHIPS
• HAWAII

EDDIE AIKAU   BILLY HAMILTON
BEN AIPA   FRED HEMMINGS
JIM BLEARS   BARRY KANAIAUPUNI
JOEY CABELL   JIMMY LUCAS
CORKY CARROLL   RUSTY MILLER
RYAN DOTSON   FELIPE POMAR
GEORGE DOWNING   PAUL STRAUCH
MIKE DOYLE   JOCK SUTHERLAND *DEFENDING CHAMPION
JACKIE EBERLE   MIKE TURKINGTON
CHARLIE GALANTO   BRUCE VALLUZZI
RICKY GRIGG   BUTCH VAN ARTSDALEN
JEFF HAKMAN   NAT YOUNG

**FOURTH ANNUAL
DEC. 17-20, 1968**
HEADQUARTERS: HILTON HAWAIIAN VILLAGE

4th Annual Duke Kahanamoku Invitational Surfing Championship poster, 1968, printed paper. Collection of Dan Pincetich

47

From left to right:
Hawaiian surfrider statue, chrome plated metal. Collection of Dan Pincetich

Trophy with redwood surfboard. Collection of Dan Pincetich

Trophy with redwood surfboard. Collection of Dan Pincetich

Swim Wear

Moana Hotel Baths swim suit, 1920s,
wool. Collection of Dan Pincetich

49

Left: Swim suit, Jantzen, 1920s, wool. Collection of Dan Pincetich

Right: Swim suit, Jantzen, 1920s, wool. Collection of Dan Pincetich

50

Rescue float, "Tom Blake Hollow Surf-board," c.1920s, Wood, metal, rope. Collection of the Santa Cruz Surfing Museum

Above: Duke Kahanamoku brand swim trunks for Outrigger Canoe Club, 1950s, cotton. Collection of Dan Pincetich

Right: Swim trunks for Outrigger Canoe Club, 1950s, cotton. Collection of Dan Pincetich

51

Greg Noll at the Banzai Pipeline, Hawai`i, photographed
by John Severson, 1963. Collection of Greg Noll

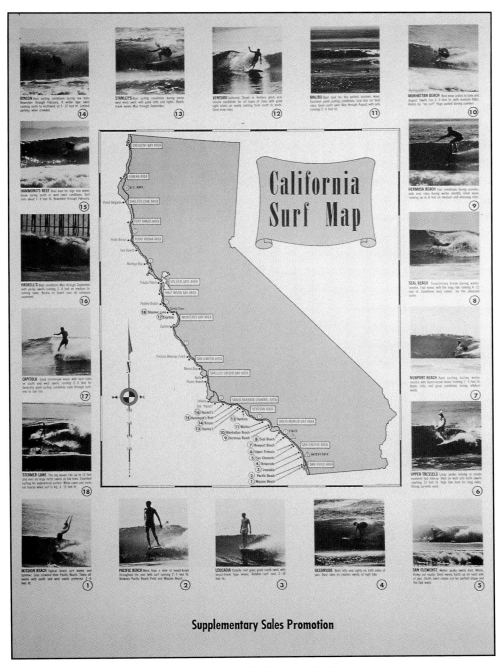

Surfing map of California, 1960s.
Collection of Cary B. Weiss

Surfing Southern California

"I shall never forget the impression which our first landing on the beach of California [at Santa Barbara] made upon me. The sun had just gone down; it was getting dusky; the damp night wind was beginning to blow, and the heavy swell of the Pacific was setting in, and breaking in loud and high 'combers' upon the beach...dusky Sandwich Islanders...gave a shout and taking advantage of a great comber which came swelling in, rearing its head...they gave three or four long and strong pulls, and went in on top of the great wave."

Richard Henry Dana, *Two Years Before the Mast*, 1834

Duke Kahanamoku

Duke Paoa Kahanamoku (1890-1968) came to southern California on his way to the 1912 Olympics, where he won a gold medal in swimming in the 100-meter freestyle. With his redwood board he astounded beach crowds at such now-famous surf spots as Santa Monica and Corona del Mar. At the time Duke was one of the world's fastest swimmers and a leading Waikiki surfer; he is still known today as the father of modern Hawaiian surfing. Duke's first trip greatly encouraged the growing body of surfers in California, and his 1915 trip to Australia had a similar impact at Freshwater Beach, Sydney. Duke spent nearly two decades in California playing bit parts in Hollywood jungle movies and did his last surfing at the age of sixty. He lived long enough to see surfing go from almost nothing to the edge of the big surfing boom in the 1960s. The first Duke Kahanamoku Invitational Surfing Championships were held at Sunset Beach, Oahu, in 1965.

According to early surf photographer John Heath "Doc" Ball, in his book *California Surfriders, 1946: A Scrapbook of Surfing and Beach Stuff,*

the best surf spots in southern California between the visit of Duke Kahanamoku in 1912 and the boom era ushered in by the 1959 movie *Gidget*, included Corona del Mar, Malibu, San Onofre, and Windansea. Some of these spots existed simultaneously; others were discovered when a favorite area was altered by construction or natural forces. By 1946, the famous Long Beach "Flood Control" was already extinct because of new breakwaters.

Surfer-inventor Bob Simmons was one of a small group of Southern Californians who helped to revolutionize surfing through new technology and design. He is credited with creating the modern surfboard. Simmons used new plastic resins and fiberglass, developed during World War II, and advanced hydrodynamic shapes. His experimental boards, made of a polystyrene foam core, balsa wood rails, a plywood deck, and bottom covered in fiberglass, were stronger and faster. This "Simmons Sandwich" represents a milestone in the evolution of the surfboard. Simmons, 1947, foam, plywood, balsa wood, fiberglass. Collection of Santa Cruz Surfing Museum

Surfboard Building

Lighter hardwoods were laminated between the outer rails of redwood giving the "Waikiki Style" boards of the 1930s their distinctive striped look. These types of surfboards, particularly the redwood models, were used in the early days of California surfing.

Above: Surfing at Palos Verdes, Dr. J. H. Ball, 1939. Collection of LeRoy Grannis and Dr. J. H. Ball

Right: Palos Verdes Surf Club, Dr. J. H. Ball, 1939. Collection of LeRoy Grannis and Dr. J. H. Ball

In the post-World War II years, California made its contribution to the sport through the use of new materials and innovative designs. Balsa wood boards had desired lightness but lacked durability. Bob Simmons, a pioneer of surfing's modern age, applied plastic and other chemicals developed during the war to surfboard making. He covered a balsa board with polyester resin and spun glass fabric. The "fiberglass" sealed and strengthened the wood and the era of the light, and durable, "Malibu" surfboard had arrived. Polyurethane then replaced wood as the core material. During the 1950s Simmons and others applied hydrodynamic principles to shaping boards that gave surfers greater maneuverability and speed.

Even in winter, Southern California water temperatures range from 55 to 57 degrees, or slightly warmer than the warmest summer temperatures in northern California. Windansea, still one of the most popular surf spots in La Jolla, was immortalized by Tom Wolfe in *The Pump House Gang*, 1968, to the dismay of many of the surfing locals.

"Better ways to build surfboards," *Popular Science Monthly Magazine*, 1935, printed paper. Collection of Dan Pincetich

Dale Velzy's shaping room, 1947, gelatin silver print. Collection of C. R. Stecyk

Tools for making surfboards: handmade wood planer, caliper, draw knives, and balsa wood shavings. Collection of C. R. Stecyk

Hobie Alter, at left, in his surfboard factory at Dana Point, California, LeRoy Grannis, 1963. Collection of LeRoy Grannis

Lorrin Harrison's barn, C. R. Stecyk, 1987, gelatin silver print. Collection of C. R. Stecyk

57

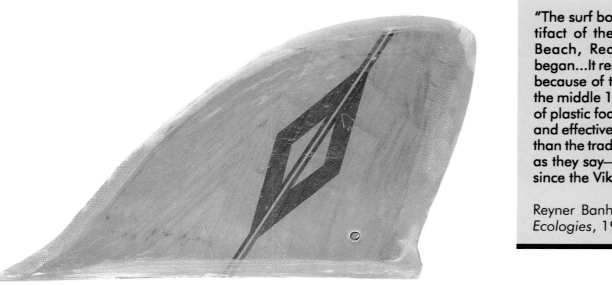

Surfboard fin, 1960s, walnut, mahogany, and fiberglass. Collection of Cary B. Weiss

Surfboard fin, Greg Noll "Da Cat" model, 1966, molded ABS. Collection of C. R. Stecyk

Surfboard fin, 1960s, ash with walnut inlay, fiberglass. Collection of Cary B. Weiss

Surfboard fin, Mike Hynson "Dolfin" model,1974, fiberglass. Collection of C. R. Stecyk

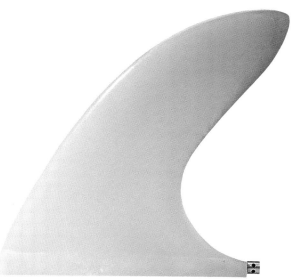

Above: Surfboard fin, Reynolds Yater #2 model, 1965, polypropelene. Collection of C. R. Stecyk

Right: Surfboard fin, Greg Noll, 1995, burlwood and resin. Collection of Noll Family Trust

Business cards of surfboard makers and decal "Murphy" logo by Rick Griffin, printed paper. Collection of Dan Pincetich

59

Design Changes

Gordon "Gordie" Duane began shaping surfboards in Compton, California in 1950. He then opened the first surf shop in Huntington Beach, California. Balsa wood boards were preferred for their lightness but the soft wood was not very durable, even when varnished. A coat of fiberglass added strength and made a surfboard impervious to water. Gordie, 1951-1954, balsa wood, fiberglass. Collection of Scott Anderson

60

Gordie price list. Collection of Cary B. Weiss

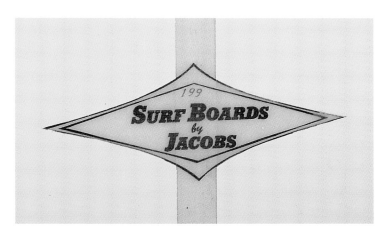

Hap Jacobs of Hermosa Beach, California, with his mentor and partner Dale Velzy, built surfboards in the 1940s and 1950s and contributed to the development of the Malibu board. Jacobs sponsored one of the most successful surfing teams of the 1960s. His surfboards of this period were made of traditional and new materials. He combined polyurethane foam and fiberglass with a two-inch wide strip, or "stringer," of balsa wood down the center. Surf Boards by Jacobs, 1960, foam, fiberglass, and balsa wood. Collection of Cary B. Weiss

Left: Bing logo decal. Collection of Cary B. Weiss

Bing Copeland, a surfer and a sailor, opened a surf shop in Hermosa Beach, California, in 1959. In 1962 over 25,000 new surfboards were purchased in California.

Underside of Keating "Delight" board by O'Neill

As surfing spots along the coast of Southern California became crowded, more emphasis was put on performance. Surfboard designs of the late 1950s and early 1960s enabled riders to execute "radical" maneuvers. The "hot dogging" style of surfing included hanging ten, drop-knee cut backs, head dips, and nose riding. Nose riding boards, with concave bottoms at the front, also known as "spoons," were popular models. Gordie Nose Rider, 1964, foam, fiberglass, and redwood. Collection of Jerry Pierce

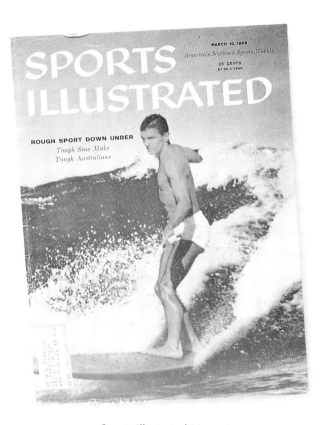

Sports Illustrated Magazine, March 10, 1958, printed paper. Collection of Cary B. Weiss

Surfing Made Easy,
by Ted Masters,
edited by Hobie
Alter, 1962, printed
paper. Collection of
the Santa Cruz
Surfing Museum

Malibu, California, LeRoy F. Grannis, 1963.
Collection of LeRoy Grannis

Hobie Alter produced this surfboard for his
team rider "Cowboy" Phil Henderson. Hobie
Surfboards of Dana Point, California, became
one of the best known, and highest volume,
manufacturers of surfboards. In 1965, Alter
invented the fin-box with a removable fin that
made traveling easier. Hobie Surfboards,
1966-1967, balsa wood and fiberglass.
Collection of Scott Anderson

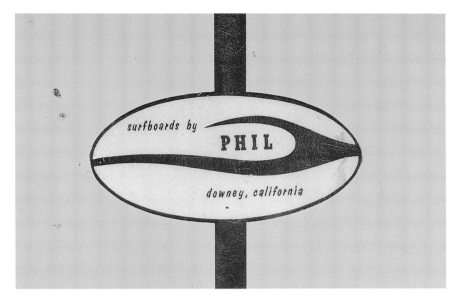

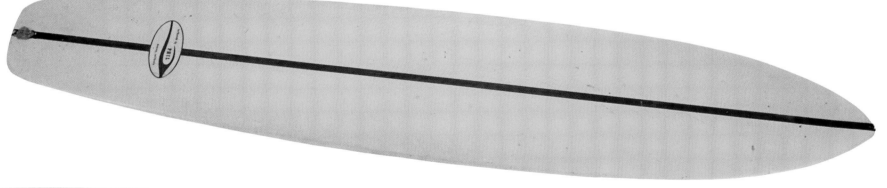

Originally produced by Dale Velzy in 1951, this surfboard re-emerged in 1964 with a coat of paint and a decal from Phil Sauers surf shop in Downey, California. It was used as a prop in the 1964 movie *Ride the Wild Surf*, and later as Sally Field's surfboard in the television series "Gidget." Designed by Velzy (Surfboards by Phil, 1963), 1951, balsa wood, fiberglass. Collection of C. R. Stecyk

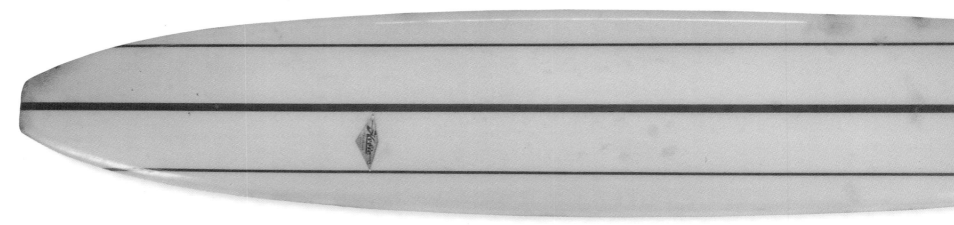

Hobie price list.
Collection of
Cary B. Weiss

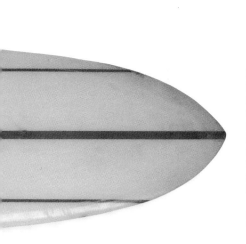

In 1963, Hobart "Hobie" Alter introduced the first signature model surfboard. Phil Edwards was well known among surfers as the first to ride the Banzai Pipeline in Hawai`i. This endorsed model features triple redwood stringers for extra strength in heavy conditions. Hobie, Phil Edwards Model, 1964, foam, fiberglass, and redwood. Collection of Cary B. Weiss

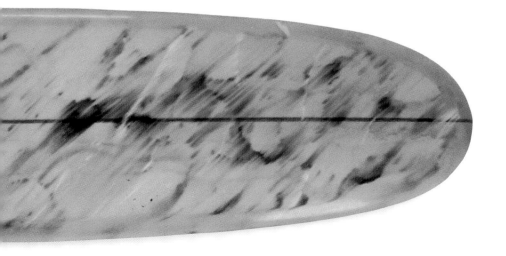

Underside of Greg Noll's "Da Cat" model, shown on page 71.

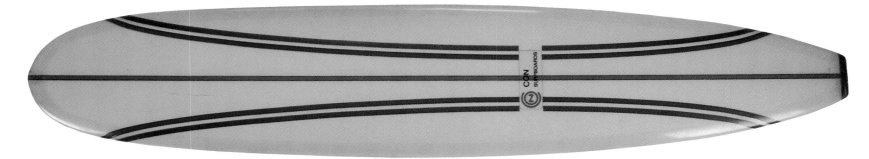

Con Surfboards, owned by Con Colburn of Santa Monica, California, sold for $85 to $100 in the seven- to twelve-foot range. His advertisements claimed, "All boards are custom built to fit each individual." Among the most popular Con surfboards was a signature model called "The Ugly," ridden by Bob Purvey. Con Surfboards, 1966-1967, foam and fiberglass. Collection of John Schell

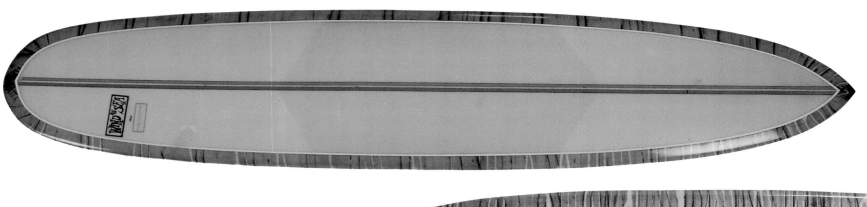

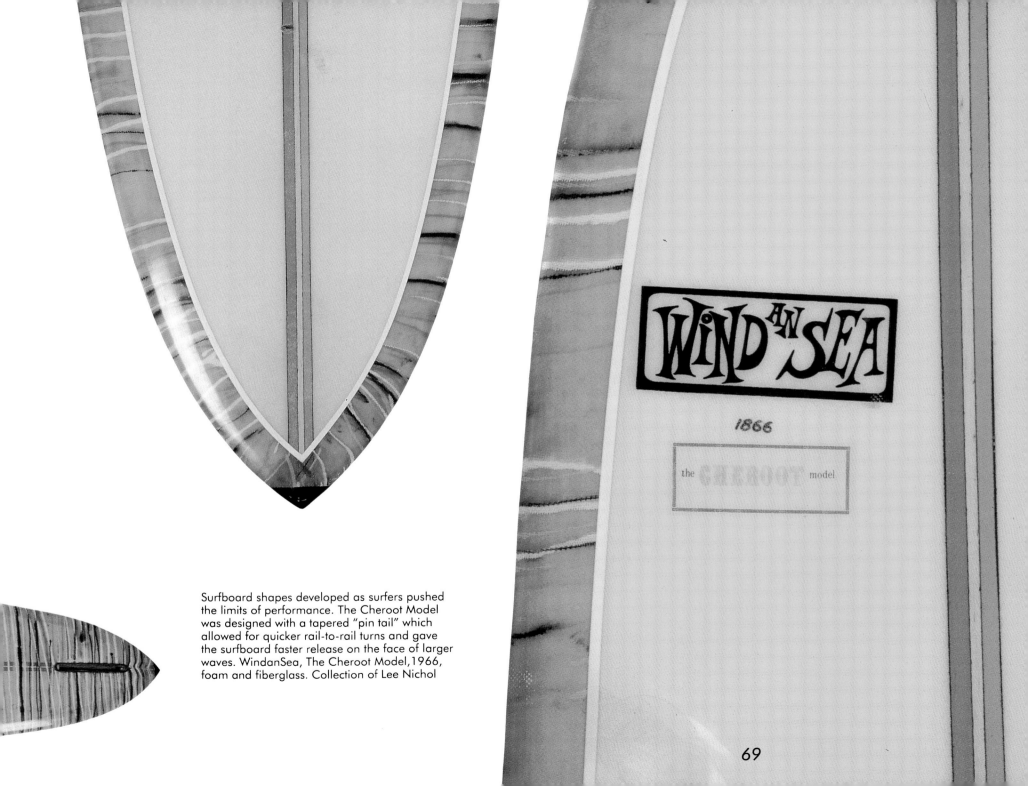

Surfboard shapes developed as surfers pushed the limits of performance. The Cheroot Model was designed with a tapered "pin tail" which allowed for quicker rail-to-rail turns and gave the surfboard faster release on the face of larger waves. WindanSea, The Cheroot Model, 1966, foam and fiberglass. Collection of Lee Nichol

WIND AN SEA

1866

the CHEROOT model

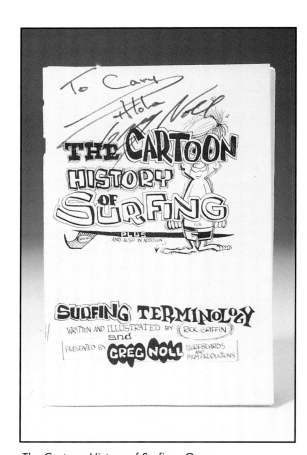

The Cartoon History of Surfing, Greg Noll and Rick Griffin, 1961, printed paper. Collection of Cary B. Weiss

Logo for Rick surfboards. Collection of Cary B. Weiss

Hooded sweatshirt, "Greg Noll Surf Boards," 1950s, fabric. Collection of Noll Family Trust

Big wave rider Greg Noll, originally from Manhattan Beach, California, was the first modern surfer known to have ridden Waimea Bay in Hawai`i. The Mickey Dora "Da Cat" Model, named for the famous Malibu surfer, was shorter and lighter than others surfboards of its time. It helped define the era of transition between longer and shorter surfboards. Greg Noll Surfboards, Mickey Dora "Da Cat" Model, c.1967, foam and fiberglass. Collection of John Schell

71

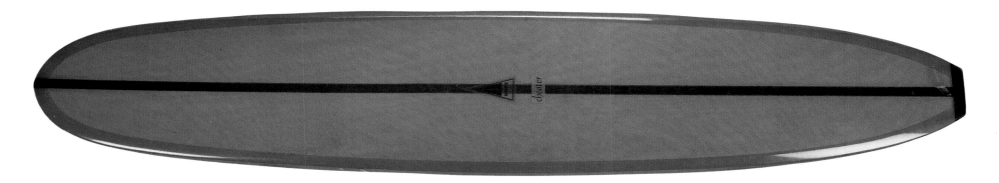

Rich Harbour of Seal Beach, California, started shaping surfboards in 1956. The "Cheater" was one of the most popular models ever produced. It was designed by Dean Elliot based on the theory that the lifted tail sets the board higher in the wave for easier nose riding. The blue tint was created by adding pigment to the resin coat. Surfboards by Harbour "Cheater," c.1967, foam, fiberglass, redwood. Collection of John Schell

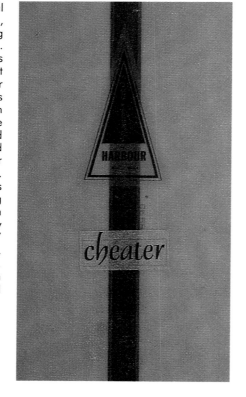

Harbour surfboards labels decal. Collection of Cary B. Weiss

72

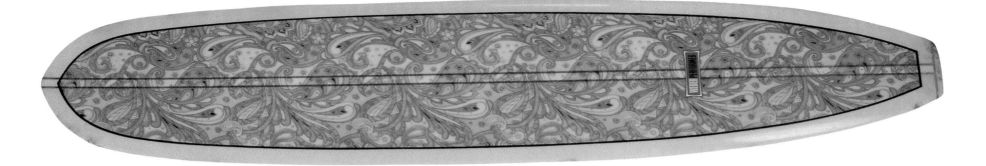

Considered the first of the contemporary hot doggers, Dewey Weber formed his own company to produce surfboards to suit his style. The Performer had a wide-scooped nose, flat bottom, and a large hatchet-shaped fin. It quickly became a popular model. Weber Performer, 1967-1968, foam and fiberglass. Collection of Lee Nichol

SURF BOARDS
by
Dewey Weber

4821 Pacific Avenue
Venice, California
EX 9-9528

Quality   *Craftsmanship*

PRICE

9'1" and under	95.00 Plus tax
9'2" to 9'6"	105.00 Plus tax
9'6" to 10'	115.00 Plus tax

THE ABOVE PRICES INCLUDE

High Density Polyurethane Foam.
Clear Finish with 20 oz. Fiberglass Cloth.
Double Layer of 20 oz. Fiberglass on Each Side of Fin.
Laminated Wood or Foam Fin with a one half inch bead.
Double Wrapped Rails and Deck Patch.
Laminated Redwood Center Strip.

EXTRAS

Extra Strips	5.00 Each
Curved Strip	3.00 Extra
Crossed Strip	3.00 Extra
2" Balsa Strip	4.00 Extra
Color	5.00 One Side
	8.00 Both Sides
Fin	4.00 Laminated Wood
	6.00 Rising Sun

DELIVERY

Approximately Two Weeks
USED BOARDS, all sizes. TRADE-INS — Value determined by age and condition. Deposits required on all orders, with balance of payment due upon delivery.
EASY FINANCING WITH APPROVED CREDIT

Dewey Weber
surfboards price
list. Collection of
Cary B. Weiss

GORDON & SMITH SURFBOARDS

Mike Hynson

PHOTO BY BRUCE BROWN

PRICE LIST

8'6" and under Tel. 488-7789	$ 95.00
8'7" to 9'0" 4650 Mission Blvd.	100.00
9'1" to 9'6"	105.00
9'7" to 10'0"	110.00

These prices include: Hand shaping by Mike Hynson or Larry Gordon, in redwood or balsa center strip, double 10-oz. glassing with Deck Patch, solid glass fin, and our guarantee of perfect craftsmanship.

EXTRAS

Laminated wood fins (your choice)	$ 5.00
Bead of fin	3.00
Balsa strip 2" wide	5.00
3" wide	10.00
1½" wide	2.50
Extra strips: redwood	5.00
balsa	10.00
Extra or multi-colored	5.00
	(each color extra)

ABOUT OUR SURFBOARDS

The reason Gordon & Smith Surfboards are considered the finest surfboards made today is seen with the first glance at their quality. First of all, a G & S is always made to your EXACT specifications. There are always perfect strips (never routed). Every G & S made is double glassed, plus a deck patch. These reasons, plus our standards of the best materials and craftsmanship, enable us to give you the best for your money. We also stand behind our surfboards 100%.

Gordon & Smith surfboards price list.
Collection of Cary B. Weiss

This surfboard, with a concave deck, was designed for riding in a kneeling position by George Greenough of Santa Barbara, California. Greenough, an influential surfer, filmmaker, and inventor, refined his surfboard designs to allow deeper positioning within the tube of a breaking wave. His designs, including new fin concepts, were instrumental in the shortboard revolution of the 1970s and in the understanding of what was possible in high performance surfing. Wilderness Surfboards, George Greenough - Designs, c.1970, foam, fiberglass. Collection of John Schell

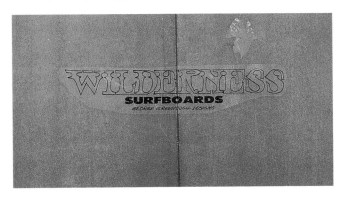

Color postcard, young girl surfing. Collection of Dan Pincetich

Above: Miniature surfboard with offset "T" band stringers, wood. Collection of Dan Pincetich

Left: Jack's Surf Shop label. Collection of Cary B. Weiss

Below: Miniature longboard, pine wood. Collection of Dan Pincetich

Foss Foam label. Collection of Cary B. Weiss

Color postcard from crowded
Hermosa Beach, California.
Collection of Dan Pincetich.

Vagabond surfboards label.
Collection of Cary B. Weiss

Miniature longboard, Dewey
Weber, foam and fiberglass.
Collection of Dan Pincetich

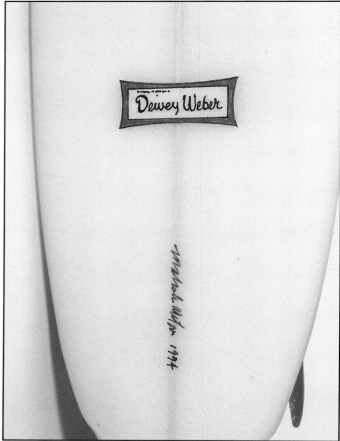

Miniature Dewey Weber
Tri-fin surfboard, foam
and fiberglass, 1994.
Collection of Dan
Pincetich

Logo for Carbonell Surf Shop,
Long Beach, California.
Collection of Cary B. Weiss

Logo for San Onofre Surfing Club,
1980. Collection of Cary B. Weiss

Color postcard from Malibu Beach,
California. Collection of Dan Pincetich

Color postcard of
surfing fun. Collection
of Dan Pincetich

Swimwear

"There are uncounted millions of people right now who are going through life without any sort of real, vibrant kick. The legions of the unjazzed. But surfers have found one way. God knows, there are other ways. Each to his own special danger. Skiing is not enough. Sailing is near. Ski jumping is almost. Automobile racing has got it. Bullfighting makes you dead. The answer is surfing."

Phil Edwards, *You Should Have Been Here an Hour Ago: The Stoked Side of Surfing or How to Hang Ten Through Life and Stay Happy*, 1967

Women with surfboards, c.1930s, gelatin silver print. Collection of Underwood Photo Archives, San Francisco

Right: Swim trunks with web belt and metal buckle, Wikies by Gantner, 1940s. Collection of the Santa Cruz Surfing Museum

Below left: Dark blue wool swim trunks with red surfer image. Collection of the Santa Cruz Surfing Museum

81

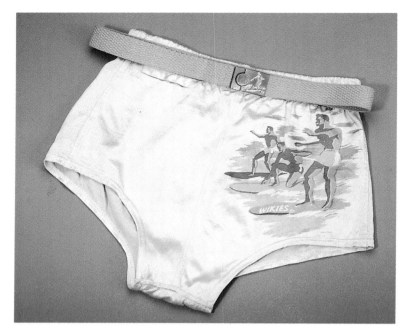

White swim trunks with colored image of surfers and web belt, Wikies by Gantner, 1940s. Collection of Dan Pincetich

Greg Noll's "Jailhouse" surf trunks, 1958, Nylon. Collection of Noll Family Trust

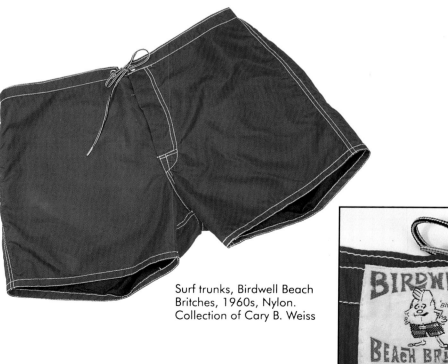

Surf trunks, Birdwell Beach Britches, 1960s, Nylon. Collection of Cary B. Weiss

Above: "Pacific Coast Championships" medallion, 1932, silver on brass. Collection of W. Babcock / Angels, Carpinteria, California

Right: Hermosa Beach, Dr. J. H. Ball, 1946. Collection of LeRoy Grannis and Dr. J. H. Ball

"It used to be a big deal if you broke a board in half—a black mark against the surfboard designer—but nowadays, guys go to the Islands and break two, three boards or more riding the winter surf because modern surfboards are lighter and slimmer."

Greg Noll, *Da Bull*, 1989

Competition

Trophy from The Santa Cruz Longboard
Union/ Club Invitational. Collection of
the Santa Cruz Surfing Museum

Photograph of the women's final competition, San Clemente, LeRoy
Grannis, 1964. Collection of LeRoy Grannis and Dr. J. H. Ball

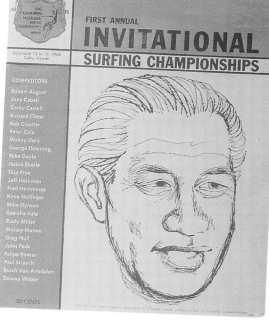

Program from the First Annual Duke Kahanamoku Invitational Surfing Championships, 1965, paper. Collection of The Keating Family

Above: Photograph of the Malibu wall, LeRoy Grannis, 1964. Collection of LeRoy Grannis and Dr. J. H. Ball

Left: WSA Surf Contest, 3rd place trophy, 1960, wood and metal. Collection of W. Babcock / Angels, Carpinteria, California

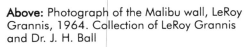

85

Logo for World Surfing Championships, San Diego, California, 1966. Collection of Cary B. Weiss

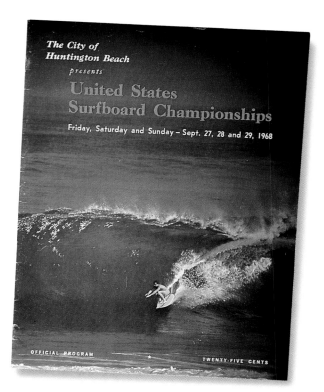

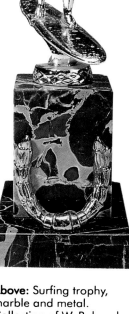

Above: United States Surfboard Championships program, 1968, printed paper. Collection of The Keating Family

Left: Huntington Beach U.S. Championship patch, 1968, cloth. Collection of The Keating Family

Above: Surfing trophy, marble and metal. Collection of W. Babcock / Angels, Carpinteria, California

Left: Western Surfing Association trophy, 1988, wood and plastic. Collection of W. Babcock / Angels, Carpinteria, California

Surfing Northern California

After Duke Kahanamoku and George Freeth brought surfing to California from Hawai`i early in this century, the sport quickly became popular along the entire California coast. Despite fog, cold weather, rain, and water temperature in the 43-55 degree range, surfers found the best breaks as far north as San Francisco and beyond. Among the most popular were Pedro Point and Shelter Cove, about 17 miles south of San Francisco in Pacifica, and Kelly Cove at Ocean Beach. Kelly's Cove is described in Bank Wright's *Surfing California: A Complete Guide to the California Coast,* 1973, as follows: "Perfect beach peaks. Breaks on any swell, 2-15 feet. Medium tide. Big and sometimes too strong during winter. Tubes spit when offshores blow out of City."

Shirley Templeman and Pat Collings with "planks" on Cowell's Beach with wharf in background, Santa Cruz, 1939. Harry Mayo Collection/Santa Cruz Surfing Museum

Above: Program for the Billy Rose Aquacade from the Golden Gate International Exposition, 1940, printed paper. Collection of The Keating Family

Below: "Uncle Dick" Keating with the Billy Rose Aquacade, 1940s, gelatin silver print. Collection of The Keating Family

Above: Shirley and Pat surfing "planks" at Cowell's Beach, Santa Cruz, 1939. Harry Mayo Collection/ Santa Cruz Surfing Museum

Right: Color postcard of beach with surfboards. Collection of Dan Pincetich

88

Two photographs of surfers at Pedro Point,
1941. Collection of The Keating Family

Pedro Point

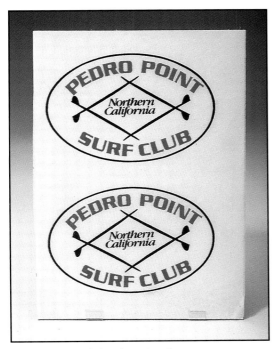

Pedro Point surf decals, printed paper.
Collection of The Keating Family

Photograph of Bob Keating surfing at Pedro Point in
the 1940s. Collection of The Keating Family

Dick Keating surfing at Pedro Point,
1940s, gelatin silver print. Collection
of The Keating Family

Dick Keating at Pedro Point, 1940s, gelatin
silver print. Collection of The Keating Family

Surfers "Uncle Dick" and Bob Keating at Pedro Point, 1940s,
gelatin silver print. Collection of The Keating Family

Jack O'Neill started a surf shop in San Francisco which he moved to Santa Cruz in 1959. He developed the wetsuit for the cold water of Northern California. In 1967 he introduced the "Delight" surfboard named for Pedro Point surfer Dick Keating who won a trophy in the prestigious Duke Kahanamoku Invitational Surfing Competition that year. Dick Keating "Delight" by O'Neill, 1967, foam, fiberglass. Richard Keating Family Collection

Left: Surfers at Pedro Point, 1940, gelatin silver print. Collection of The Keating Family

Below: Palos Verde Surf Club, Southern California, 1949. Dr. J.H. Ball. Collection of Dr. J.H. Ball

Santa Cruz

Santa Cruz is located in central California and has long been a favorite spot for surfers, who quickly found Pleasure Point and Steamer Lane along hundreds of miles of coastline notable for restricted access. The water temperature ranges from 47 degrees to 55 degrees, making full wetsuits mandatory. Bank Wright's *Surfing California: A Complete Guide to the California Coast*, 1973, recommends boots and gloves as well and cautions that the water is "cold—all year". The tide plays an important role in surfing along the central coast. It can determine whether a beach break is ridable or if a reef is safe. The "Middle Peak" of Steamer Lane breaks both winter and summer but attains its best size and shape at medium-high tide during a strong northwest swell. Pleasure Point is a series of reef breaks best in winter when the surf is strong. The shore is bordered by steep cliffs and rocks.

Dave "Count" Littlefield wearing an original "Santa Cruz surfing club" tee shirt, Santa Cruz, 1938. Harry Mayo Collection\Santa Cruz Surfing Museum

Board house on the cliff at Cowell's Beach, Santa Cruz, where the Santa Cruz Surfing Club kept their boards, 1939. Harry Mayo Collection/Santa Cruz Surfing Museum

The Woody

The woody, or woodie, is a vintage wooden-paneled, surfboard carrying station wagon. The vehicle, which also can be any old car used by surfers to haul boards to the beach, is so named because of the wood paneling used on the sides of station wagons in the 1930s, 1940s, and early 1950s.

Above: Oldsmobile Station Wagon (Woodie), 1941. Metal, wood, leather, rubber, glass. Collection of L.T. Caywoody, Restoration, San Leandro, California. Photograph by Catherine Buchanan, Courtesy San Francisco Airport Museums

Left: Group of surfers and their woodies at Cowell's Beach checking out the surf, 1941, Santa Cruz. Harry Mayo Collection/Santa Cruz Surfing Museum

95

DON
PATERSON

HARRY
MURRY

RICH
THOMPSON

ALEX
HOKAMP

BLAKE
TURNER

BILL
GRACE

BUSTER
STEWARD

FRED
HUNT

HARRY
MAYO

PINKY
PEDEMONTE

Santa Cruz
Surfing
Club
"Butter"
CUP
Sucker
"watch your
step"
TOMMY
ROUSSELL
Don't Stand
HERE
you may
Fall

SANTA CRUZ SURFING CLUB
JUNE, 1941

Above: Photograph of eleven men standing in front of their surfboards, 1941. Collection of the Santa Cruz Surfing Museum

Opposite: Photograph of the Santa Cruz Surfing Club at Cowell's Beach before the hotel was built on the cliff, 1941. Harry Mayo Collection/Santa Cruz Surfing Museum

96

Above: Record album "Surf Beat '80," with woody prominent. Collection of Cary B. Weiss

Above right: Photograph of two waves in the surf. Collection of the Santa Cruz Surfing Museum

Right Members of the Santa Cruz Surfing Club sitting on their surfboards at Cowell's Beach, Santa Cruz, 1941. Harry Mayo Collection/Santa Cruz Surfing Museum

Facing page: Photograph of nine surfers kneeling on their surfboards, 1940s. Collection of the Santa Cruz Surfing Museum

Embroidered patch, "West Wind Surf Club, Santa Cruz County." Collection of the Santa Cruz Surfing Museum

Embroidered patch "Johnny Rice Custom Surfboards, Santa Cruz." Collection of the Santa Cruz Surfing Museum

Logo decal of "Surfboards by Olson, Santa Cruz." Collection of Santa Cruz Surfing Museum

Logo decal of "Scofield Surfboards, Santa Cruz, California." Collection of Santa Cruz Surfing Museum

San Francisco

Photograph of the first surf shop in San Francisco located across from Fleishacker pool, gelatin silver print. Collection of the Santa Cruz Surfing Museum

Photograph of the second surf shop in San Francisco, located at Ocean Beach, 1950s, gelatin silver print. Collection of the Santa Cruz Surfing Museum

Left: John Sherry and Danny Elber, Kelly's Cove, San Francisco, 1965. Collection of John Sherry

Below: Ocean Beach, San Francisco, 1970s, Ross Adami. Collection of Ross Adami

Pier at Ocean Beach, San Francisco, Ross Adami,
1968, gelatin silver print. Collection of Ross Adami

105

Newspaper article "Pollution Laps at Surfers" at
Ocean Beach. Collection of Ross Adami

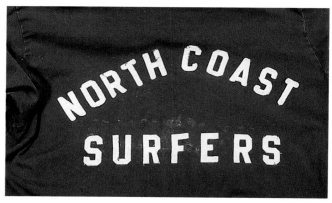

106

Left: Wind breaker
jacket, "North Coast
Surfers," 1950s,
fabric. Collection of
The Keating Family

Facing page: North
Coast Surfers Club,
1960s, gelatin silver
print. Collection of
The Keating Family

William Hickey started shaping surfboards in his garage in the Sunset District of San Francisco in the late 1960s. The powerful waves and colder water of Northern California added to the challenges faced by surfers. Hickey Custom Surfboards, c.1969, foam and fiberglass. Collection of Santa Cruz Surfing Museum

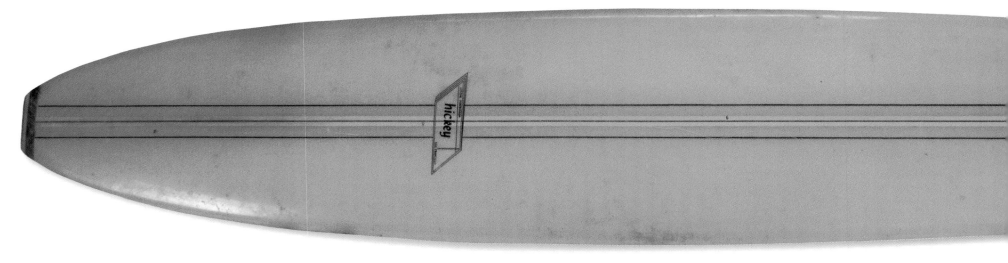

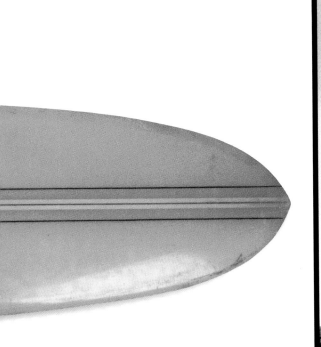

Left: Embroidered patch "Exhibition Team." Collection of the Santa Cruz Surfing Museum

Below: Photograph of three men, including Barrington and Freitas, one wearing a jacket lettered "Surfrider" at Ocean Beach, San Francisco, 1967. Collection of John Sherry

109

Wetsuits

"Trunkin' it" (wearing only surf trunks while surfing—no wetsuit) may be a good idea in Hawai`i where the water temperature is 76 degrees, but in central and northern California where the water temperature can range from 43 to 55 degrees, protection from the cold is a necessity. In the 1950s wetsuits were pioneered by Jack O'Neill at Ocean Beach, San Francisco, where the water is cold year round. He experimented by wearing sweaters out in the ocean, then navy jackets sprayed with Thompson's water seal, and later, unicellular foam. Today's wetsuit is a neoprene rubber suit, usually 1/8 inch thick. The seams are glued together, or sometimes glued and stitched. The suits are designed to fit snugly, but to allow a thin layer of water to enter, so that the water can be warmed by body heat and keep the user warm. In Southern California, where summer water temperatures can rise into the 70s, wetsuits are an effective barrier against jellyfish.

O'Neill prototype wetsuit, "Original Vest," O'Neill, 1950s, uni-cellular foam and rubber. Collection of O'Neill

110

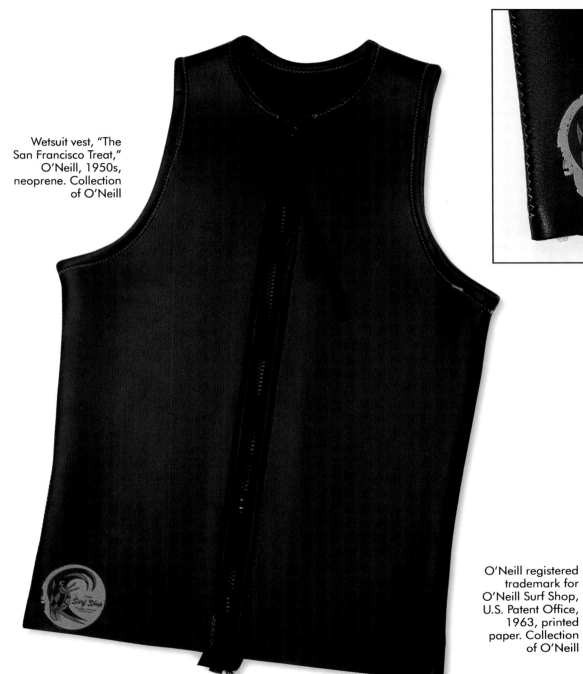

Wetsuit vest, "The San Francisco Treat," O'Neill, 1950s, neoprene. Collection of O'Neill

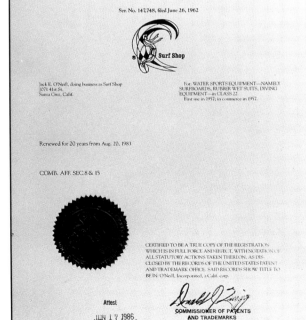

O'Neill registered trademark for O'Neill Surf Shop, U.S. Patent Office, 1963, printed paper. Collection of O'Neill

Above: O'Neill trademark, printed paper.
Collection of O'Neill

Right: John Sherry and Bob Steers on the
surf, 1967. Collection of John Sherry

Child's "beaver tail"
wetsuit top, O'Neill
Wetsuits, 1950s,
neoprene. Collection
of O'Neill

"Beaver tail" wetsuit top, Sea suits of California—The Bod Pod, Neoprene. Collection of the Santa Cruz Surfing Museum

Wetsuit top, "San Francisco Surf Shop," 1960s, neoprene. Collection of the Santa Cruz Surfing Museum

114

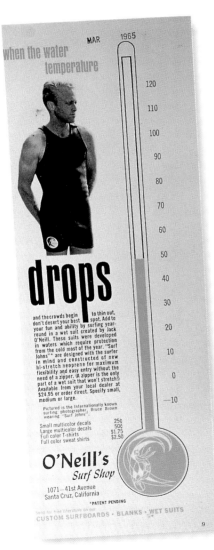

Above: Bob Steers and John Sherry at Kelly's
Cove, San Francisco, 1970s, Ross Adami.
Collection of Ross Adami

Left: Advertisment for O'Neill wetsuits, 1965.
Collection of O'Neill

Wetsuit "ZEN,"
Zipperless Entry
Neck, c.1990s,
O'Neill, neoprene
rubber. Collection
of O'Neill

Decal of "Western Surfing Association 1970."
Collection of Cary B. Weiss

Sign for California
Surf Lifesaving
Association. Collection
of Cary B. Weiss

116

O'Neill Woman's "beaver tail" wetsuit top,
1968, neoprene. Collection of W. Babcock
/ Angels, Carpinteria, California

"Uncle Dick's Surfest II" trophy, won by Shona Keating,
1996, Wood, laminate. Collection of The Keating Family

Kelly's Cove, San
Francisco, 1970s,
Ross Adami. Collec-
tion of Ross Adami

Surfing in Advertising

San Francisco,
Cal.
U.S.A.
April 24/02
Arrived allright.
Letter also coming by this mail.
R.B. Turner.

By the 1920s, surfing images were used in advertisements, not just for Hawai`i, with descriptive slogans such as "In the Water or Out, it's Cool all Summer in Hawai`i," but for unlikely products such as Valspar varnish and Gossard Corsets. The associations with youth, freedom, freshness, balance, and a host of other concepts were irresistible to advertisers. By the 1950s, Schaeffer pens and pencils, Pontiac automobiles, and Kelly Springfield Tires had joined the list of consumer items made more attractive by references to surfing.

Postcard, 1902,
printed paper.
Collection of Dan
Pincetich

Above: Color postcard, "Lone Surfer," 1910. Collection of J. & M. Ford

Above right: Private mailing card No. 16, "On the Beach at Waikiki," 1915, paper. Collection of Dan Pincetich

Right: Booklet, "Aloha Honolulu Hawaiian Islands," Hart and Company. Collection of J. & M. Ford

120

World Outlook Magazine, May, 1920,
printed paper. Collection of J. & M. Ford

Travel brochure,
printed paper.
Collection of J. & M.
Ford

"Surfing is the art of harnessing that ocean energy,
and in doing that the surfer momentarily becomes a
sea creature, moving in rapport with the waves."

Richard Wolkomir, *Oceans Magazine*, June, 1988

Valspar varnish advertisement in *The Saturday Evening Post*, 1922, printed paper. Collection of Dan Pincetich.

Above: Pleasanton Hotel brochure, 1920s, printed paper. Collection of Dan Pincetich

Right: Advertisement for Gossard Corsets, *Vogue Magazine*, May, 1926. Collection of Dan Pincetich

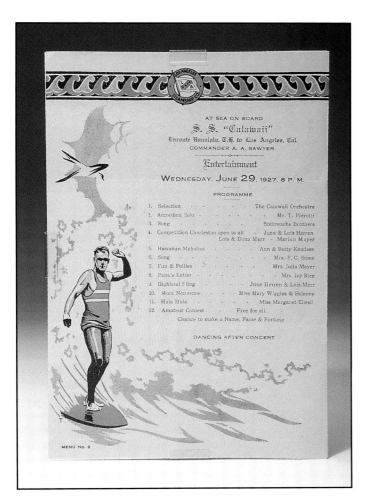

Above: S.S. Calawaii program, 1927, printed paper. Collection of Dan Pincetich

Right: Color printed "Souvenir Passenger List," c. 1920s, printed paper. Collection of Dan Pincetich

Above & facing page: Brochure, Los Angeles Steamship Co., 1920s, printed paper. Collection of Dan Pincetich

125

Left: Hawaii Tourist Bureau advertisement from *Country Life*, 1929, printed paper. Collection of Dan Pincetich.

Above: Booklet, *Hawaiian Islands*, 1929, printed paper. Collection of Dan Pincetich

Right: Advertisement for Shaeffer's pens and pencils, *The Liberty Digest*, August 30, 1930. Collection of Dan Pincetich

Above: Advertisement, Hawaii Tourist Bureau, 1930, printed paper. Collection of Dan Pincetich

Left: Booklet, *Hawaii, The Paradise of the Pacific*, printed paper. Collection of J. & M. Ford

Dole Pineapple Juice advertisement, 1938, printed paper. Collection of Dan Pincetich

Vogue Magazine, December 15, 1938, paper. Collection of Dan Pincetich

First day of issue postage envelope, 1937, printed paper. Collection of Dan Pincetich

> "The funny thing is, I think I laughed...it was so unbelievable. It was like a cartoon almost."

Mark Foo, surfer, recalling an encounter with a fifty-foot wave

Advertisement for Matson Line ships, 1939, printed paper. Collection of Dan Pincetich

Light hearts make buoyant riding over the surf at Waikiki

Details of *Matson Cruises to Hawaii and South Seas*, also *reservations* at the Royal Hawaiian and Moana Hotels in Honolulu, from any Travel Agent or from MATSON LINE offices at New York, Chicago, San Francisco, Los Angeles, San Diego, Seattle and Portland.

This Year . . . SAN FRANCISCO'S WORLD'S FAIR . . . *Then* HAWAII

Matson Line
TO *Hawaii* · NEW ZEALAND · AUSTRALIA
VIA SAMOA · FIJI

S. S. LURLINE · S. S. MARIPOSA · S. S. MONTEREY · S. S. MATSONIA

Luggage tag, "Matson Navigation Co., Honolulu, Surf-riding," plastic and leather. Collection of J. & M. Ford

Swimsuits Advertisement, Jantzen, *Saturday Evening Post*, 1938, printed paper. Collection of Dan Pincetich

Above: Vitalized Ginger Ale sign, 1940s, metal. Collection of Dan Pincetich

Right: "Riding the Surf in Hawaii," *Collier's Outdoor America*, July, 1944, printed paper. Collection of Dan Pincetich

Kelly Springfield Tires advertisement, 1940s, printed paper. Collection of Dan Pincetich

Pennant, "Aloha," fabric.
Collection of J. & M. Ford

Label for Sunny Scene Brand Beets, 1950. Collection of Dan Pincetich

Above & left: Hind Clarke Dairy milk bottle with surfer, glass. Collection of Dan Pincetich

"Hi Ball Punch" Liberty Orange Soda beverage bottle, 1950s, glass. Collection of Dan Pincetich

133

Above: Surf Rider Okolehao bottle, Bottled by Hawaiian Distillers, polychrome ceramic. Collection of J. & M. Ford

Lerft: Mobil oil advertisement, 1958, printed paper. Collection of Dan Pincetich

Above: *Hawaiian Surfriding, The Ancient and Royal Pastime,* Tom Blake, 1961, printed paper. Collection of Mark Renneker, M.D.

Right: Pontiac automobile advertisement, 1958, printed paper. Collection of Dan Pincetich

Surfing Music & Films

The California surfin' sound was instrumental (Dick Dale, the Belairs) or vocal (The Beach Boys, Jan and Dean) and its impact was tremendous. As Al Jardine said, "I think we had a lot to do with the population rush to California. People hearing The Beach Boys songs envisioned California as a sort of a golden paradise where all you did was surf and sun yourself while gorgeous blondes rubbed coconut oil on your body." Among the most memorable song titles were "Surfin' Safari," "Pipeline," and "Wipe Out."

Miniature surfboard ticket, "S.M. Surf Club 6th Annual Hawaiian Dance, 1939, wood. Collection of Cary B. Weiss

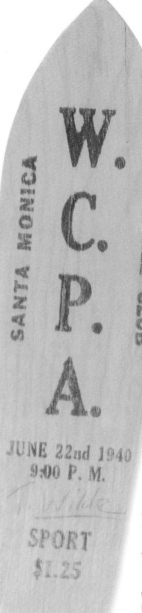

Miniature surfboard ticket, "W.C.P.A. (West Coast Paddling Association) Dance at S.M. Deauville Club," 1940, wood. Collection of Cary B. Weiss

THE BEACH BOYS
WHEN I GROW UP (to be a man)
SHE KNOWS ME TOO WELL

Capitol RECORDS 5245

"Catch a wave and you're sittin' on top of the world."

Brian Wilson, The Beach Boys, 1962

45 rpm record player, RCA,
c.1950s, plastic and metal.
Collection of Gary Saxon -
The Record Man

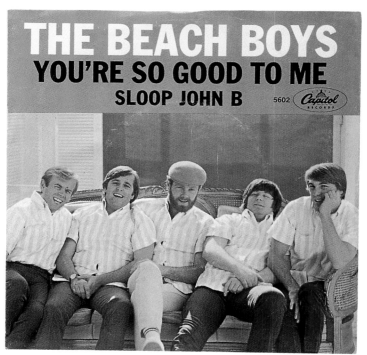

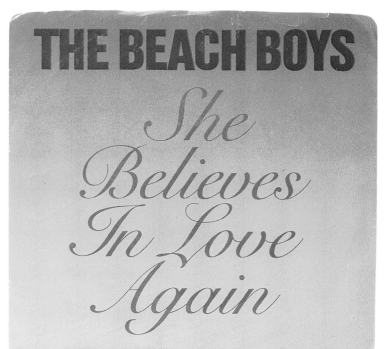

Top left: Record album jacket, "When I Grow Up, She Knows Me Too Well," The Beach Boys. Collection of Gary Saxon - The Record Man

Top right: Record album jacket, "California Girls, Let Him Run Wild," The Beach Boys. Collection of Gary Saxon - The Record Man

Bottom left: Record album jacket, "You're So Good To Me," The Beach Boys. Collection of Gary Saxon - The Record Man

Botton right: Record album jacket, "She Believes In Love Again," The Beach Boys. Collection of Gary Saxon - The Record Man

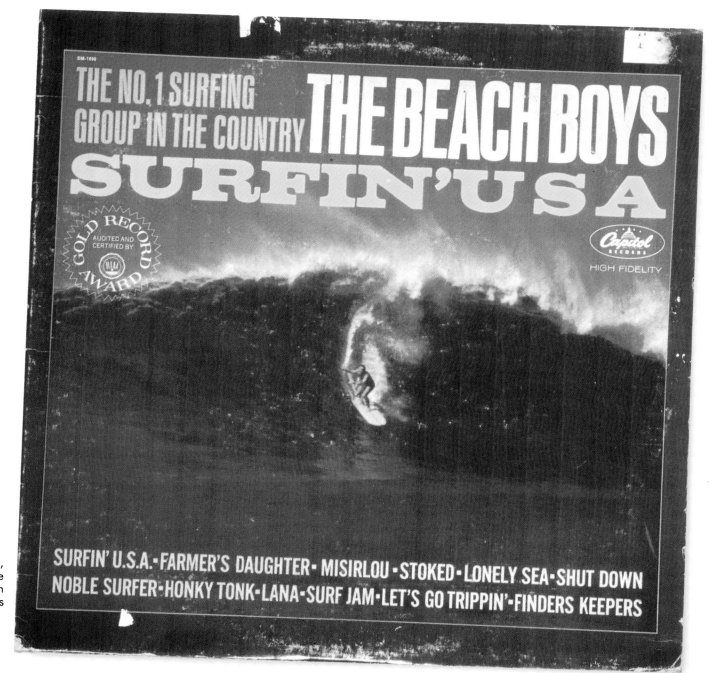

Record album jacket,
"Surfin' USA," The
Beach Boys. Collection
of Cary B. Weiss

STEREO   GS 1433

GUEST STAR

the
**beach
boys
surfaris
dick
dale
surf kings**

LATIN SOUL

DELANO SOUL BEAT

SURFIN

SURFIN' DANCE

BIG BOARD

NIGHT SURF PARTY

SURF WATER

WHITE CAP

THE FAIREST OF THEM ALL

WE'LL NEVER HEAR THE END OF IT

Record album
jacket, "Safaris,"
The Beach Boys
and Dick Dale.
Collection of Cary
B. Weiss

140

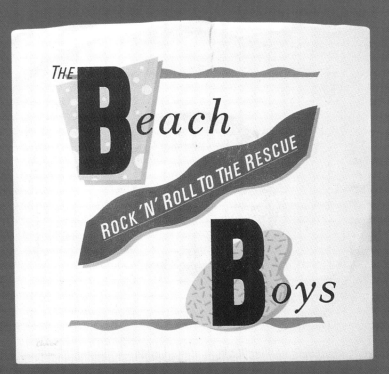

SURFER GIRL · CATCH A WAVE · THE SURFER MOON · SOUTH BAY SURFER · HAWAII
IN MY ROOM · THE ROCKING SURFER · SURFER'S RULE · YOUR SUMMER DREAM · BOOGIE WOODIE

Above: Record album jacket, "Surfer Girl," The Beach Boys. Collection of Cary B. Weiss

Above left: Record album jacket, "Rock an Roll to the Rescue," The Beach Boys. Collection of Gary Saxon - The Record Man

Left: Record album jacket, "Getcha Back," The Beach Boys. Collection of Gary Saxon - The Record Man

141

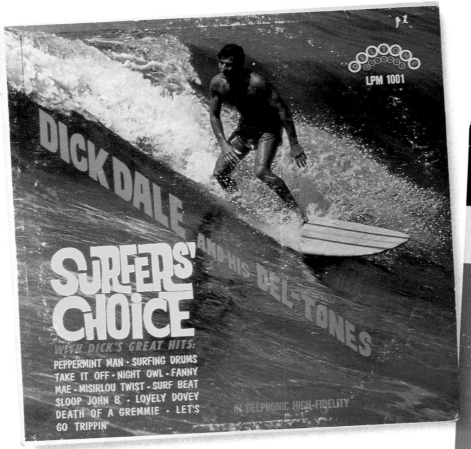

Above: Record album jacket, "The Surfers' Choice," Dick Dale and his Del-Tones. Collection of Cary B. Weiss

Right: Record album jacket, "Jan and Dean take Linda Surfin'." Collection of Cary B. Weiss

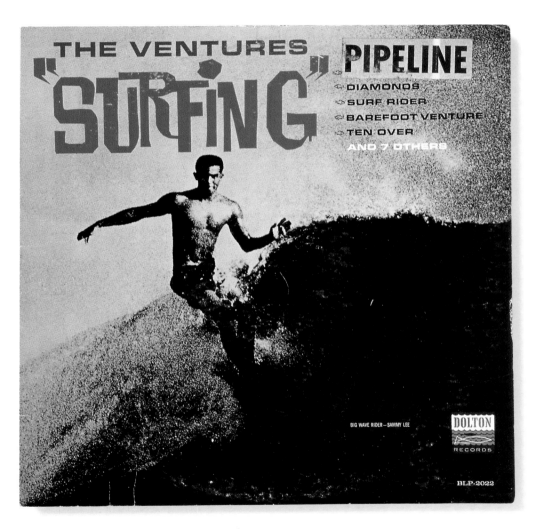

Above: Record album jacket, "Surf City," Jan and Dean. Collection of Cary B. Weiss

Left: Record album jacket, "Surfing," The Ventures. Collection of Cary B. Weiss

yikes!
IT'S ON COLORED VINYL!

File Under: The Tornadoes Surf /Instrumental Groups   LP 5024

BUSTIN' SURFBOARDS
THE TORNADOES

sundazed
LP 5024

Record album jacket, "Bustin' Surf Sounds,"
The Tornadoes. Collection of Cary B. Weiss

Vista
BV-3327

ANNETTE Sings
GOLDEN SURFIN' HITS
SIDEWALK SURFIN'
SURFER'S STOMP
SURFIN' U.S.A.
SURFER BOY
SURF CITY
SURFIN' SAFARI
RIDE THE WILD SURF
BALBOA BLUE
BOY TO LOVE
JUST STRICTLY SURFIN'
NO ONE COULD BE PROUDER

and just for fun
"THE MONKEY'S UNCLE"

Left: Record album
jacket, "Annette
Sings Surfing Hits,"
Collection of Cary
B. Weiss

Below: Record
album jacket,
"Wipeout and Surfer
Joe," The Surfaris.
Collection of Cary B.
Weiss

STEREO
DLP 25835
THE SURFARIS
THE ORIGINAL HIT VERSIONS!
ULTRA HIGH-FIDELITY
Dot
RECORDS
WIPE OUT
AND
SURFER JOE
AND OTHER POPULAR SELECTIONS BY OTHER INSTRUMENTAL GROUPS

144

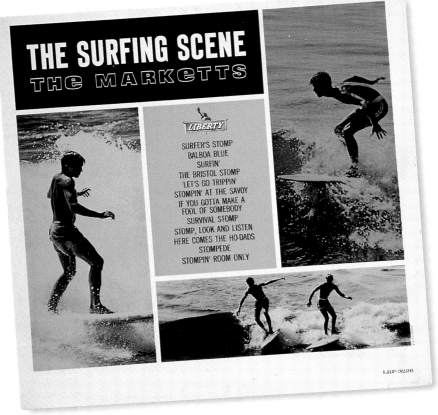

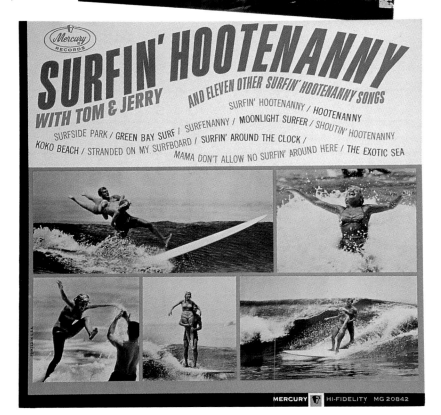

Right: Record album jacket, "Surfin' Wild." Collection of Cary B. Weiss

Below: Record album jacket, "Surfin' Hootenanny" with Tom & Jerry. Collection of Cary B. Weiss

Record album jacket, "The Surfing Scene," The Larkettes. Collection of Cary B. Weiss

"Surfing's been a real trendsetter—surf music, fashion, even the lingo. You know, terms that were developed on the beach to describe waves and rides and other surfers you end up hearing on sitcoms a year later, like 'dweeb.' I've heard that word a hundred times on TV, but I made it up a buncha years ago."

Corky Carroll, 1989

145

PRAY FOR SURF

THE PACKARDS

SURFSIDE
001 STEREO

Record album jacket,
"Pray For Surf," The
Packards. Collection
of Cary B. Weiss

146

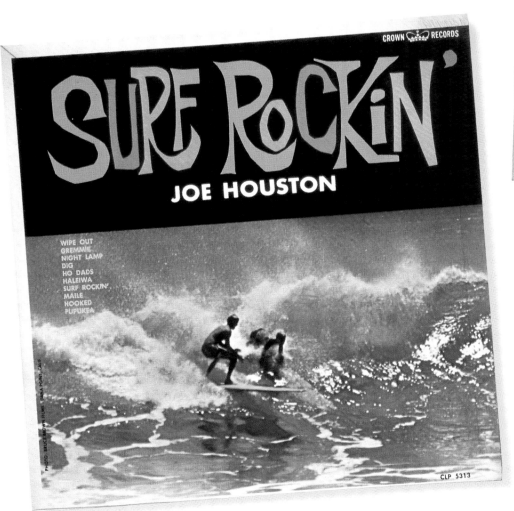

WIPE OUT
GREMMIE
NIGHT LAMP
DIG
HO DADS
HALEIWA
SURF ROCKIN'
MAILE
HOOKED
PUPUKEA

CLP 5313

Record album jacket, "Surf Rockin'," Joe Houston. Collection of Cary B. Weiss

RED RIVER ROCK
HOT AND GLASSY
SURFERS BEAT
GREEN SLEEVES AND BLUE BAGGIES
WHEN THE KOOKS GO SURFIN BY
FOAM AND FIBERGLASS
QUEENS SURF
WOODIE
ROMPIN AT RINCON
WIPE OUT AT SUNSET BEACH

CLP 5312

Left: Record album jacket, "Surfers Beat," Mike Adams and the Red Jackets. Collection of Cary B. Weiss

Below: Record album jacket, "Freddy King Does Surfin'." Collection of Cary B. Weiss

freddy king
KING 856
Goes SURFIN'

THE HITS

Hide Away...The Stumble...San-Ho-Zay...Swooshy...Butterscotch...Side Tracked
Sen-Sa-Shun...Wash Out...In The Open...Heads Up...Just Pickin'...Out Front

VIVID SOUND

147

Record album jacket, "Surf Stompin'," Don Dailey. Collection of Cary B. Weiss

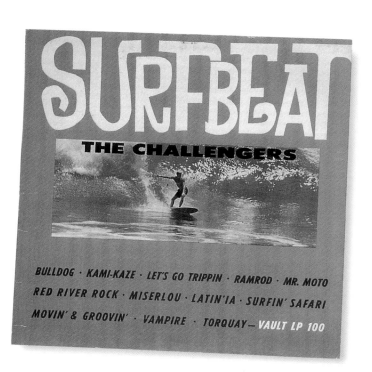

Record album jacket, "Surfbeat," The Challengers. Collection of Cary B. Weiss

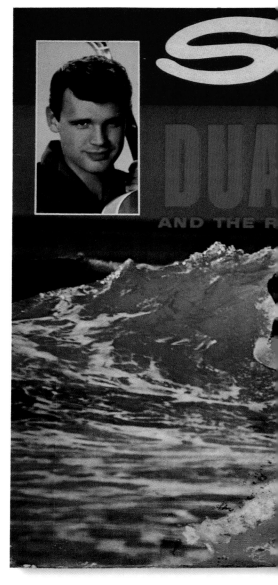

Record album jacket, "Surfin'," Duane Eddy. Collection of Cary B. Weiss

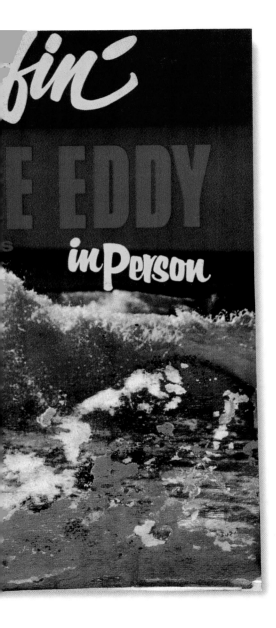

Record album jacket, "Barefoot Adventure,"
Bud Shank. Collection of Cary B. Weiss

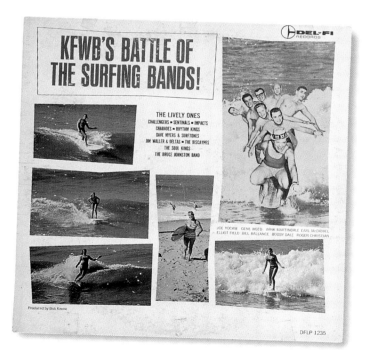

Record album jacket, "KFBW's Battle of the
Surfing Bands!" Collection of Cary B. Weiss

SURF'S UP!

THE CHALLENGERS ON TV

MR. MOTO '65 ■ APACHE '65

WIPE OUT '65 ■ THEME FROM "SURF'S UP"

PIPELINE '65 ■ K-39

KAMI KAZE '65 ■ TORQUAY ■ CHANNEL NINE

MOONDAWG ■ FOOTAPPER

ROSS AT SUNSET ■ CHIFLADO '65

THEME FROM "THE ADVENTURES
OF DELVY McNORT"

STAN RICHARDS host of the top-rated "Surf's Up" TV Show on
KHJ-TV Channel 9 Los Angeles, California ■ featuring The Challengers

VAULT RECORDS

Record album jacket,
"Surf's Up," The
Challengers on TV.
Collection of Cary B.
Weiss

OCTOBER, 1924

PRICE 20 CENTS

FILM FUN

"THE SEA HAWK"

Surfing Films

Hollywood's version of the surf culture led to such films as *Gidget*, 1959; *Beach Party*, 1963; and *Ride the Wild Surf*, 1964, with the title song by Jan and Dean, all centering heavily on teenage romance. Independently made surf movies include feature-length documentaries such as Bruce Brown's *The Endless Summer*, 1964, with the sound track by the Sandals, which followed two surfers around the world in their search for the perfect wave.

Film Fun Magazine,
October, 1924,
printed paper.
Collection of Dan
Pincetich

Gidget

THE LITTLE GIRL WITH BIG IDEAS

a novel by
FREDERICK KOHNER

Kahuna: "I'm a surf bum. You know, ride the waves, eat, sleep, not a care in the world."

Gidget: "It may be awfully nosy of me, but when do you work?"

Kahuna: "I tried that once, but there were too many hours and rules and regulations....For them," [he says of Moondoggie and the others] "it's a summer romance. For me, it's a full-time passion."

Dialogue from surf movie *Gidget*, 1959

Gidget, Frederick Kohner, Van Rees Press, New York, 1957, made into a movie of major significance in the surfing world. Collection of Mark Renneker, M.D.

Movie poster *Slippery When Wet*, Bud Shank, 1958, with opening dates for Pasadena and Santa Monica showings.

Above: Ticket for a showing of the film *Slippery When Wet*, presented by Velzy & Jacobs Surfboard Company.

Below: Record album jacket for the soundtrack to *Slippery When Wet*, Bud Shank. Collection of Cary B. Weiss

Above: Record album jacket for the soundtrack to *Golden Breed*, The Back Wash Rhythm Band. Collection of Cary B. Weiss

Right: Poster for Severson Studios present *Surf Safari*, 1959.

> "Surfing affects your lifestyle like no other sport I know of...The surf is only good at certain times...If you are a serious surfer, you have to design your life around it."

Mike Doyle, former pro surfer, *Morning Glass*

Movie projector, 1960s, metal. Collection of Jim and Mary-Lou McDonald. 8mm surf movie box, *Hawaii's Big Surf*, John Severson, 1960s, printed paper. Collection of W. Babcock / Angels, Carpinteria, California

Poster for Bruce Brown Films *Surfing Hollow Days*. Collection of Cary B. Weiss

155

SANTA MONICA CIVIC AUDITORIUM
FRIDAY, AUGUST 25   8:15 P.M.

LAST SHOWING IN L.A. – SANTA MONICA OF BIG WEDNESDAY

JOHN SEVERSON'S 1961 COLOR SURF ADVENTURE

Above: Filmmaker Bruce Brown at Malibu, California, LeRoy F. Grannis, 1963. Collection of LeRoy Grannis

Left: Poster for the film *Have Board Will Travel*, 1963. Collection of Cary B. Weiss

Facing page: Poster for the film *Big Wednesday*, 1961. Collection of Cary B. Weiss

STOKED: To catch a wave was (and is) to stoke the fires of the heart and soul; hence the terms: to be stoked, the stoked life, degrees of stoke, and pure stoke.

John Grissom, *Pure Stoke*, 1982

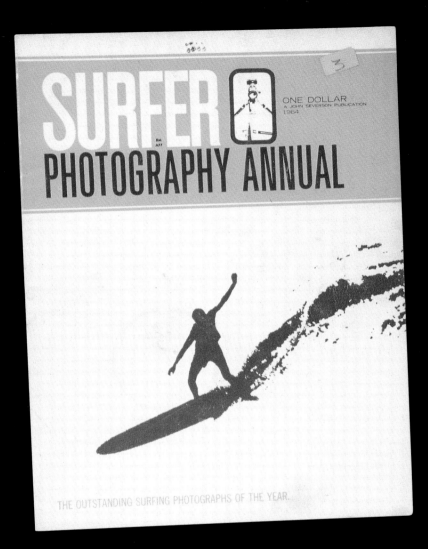

STEREO GR-7720

HONK

The Original Sound Track from

FIVE SUMMER STORIES

A FILM BY GREG MACGILLIVRAY AND JIM FREEMAN

Above: Surfer Photography Annual magazine, November, 1964, Printed paper. Collection of Cary B. Weiss

Right: Record album jacket for the soundtrack to the film Honk, Five Summer Stories. Collection of Cary B. Weiss

Facing page: Record album jacket for the soundtrack to the film Muscle Beach Party, 1964. Collection of Cary B. Weiss

"Surfing attracts dedicated cultists who build their lives around their sport—but so does golf. The important distinction between the two is that no one ever stays up late to catch a great golf flick on the late show. No one cruises down Pacific Coast Highway with the radio blasting out a bitchin' golf tune. Indeed...there is something very nearly mystical about the lone surfer who spends hours bobbing atop powerful ocean swells just for the chance to thrust himself into the curl of a breaking wave for a few heartstopping moments. 'Surfing is a dance form, and the ocean is like a liquid stage,' says one veteran surfer."

Jonathan Kirsch, "Still Surfin' After All These Years," *New West*, May, 1981

RICH
THOMPSON

ALEX
HOKAMP

BLAKE
TURNER

BILL
GRACE

BUSTER
STEWARD

FRED
HUNT

HARRY
MAYO

PINKY
PEDEMONTE

TOMMY
ROUSSEL

SANTA CRUZ SURFING CLUB
JUNE, 1941